THE GRIFFIN POETRY PRIZE
Anthology 2018

House of Anansi Press is committed to protecting our natural environment.
As part of our efforts, the interior of this book is printed on paper that contains
at least 30% post-consumer waste recycled fibres and is processed chlorine-free.

22 21 20 19 18   1 2 3 4 5

Library and Archives Canada Cataloguing in Publication

Cataloguing data available from Library and Archives Canada

Library of Congress Control Number: 2018940911

Cover design: Chloé Griffin and Kyra Griffin
Cover image: *There's a Fire* by Kai McCall, 2017
Inside cover image: *Urmasse* by Simone Gilges, 2008
Typesetting: Laura Brady

*We acknowledge for their financial support of our publishing program the Canada Council for the
Arts, the Ontario Arts Council, and the Government of Canada through the Canada Book Fund.*

Printed and bound in Canada

THE GRIFFIN POETRY PRIZE

Anthology 2018

A SELECTION OF THE SHORTLIST

Edited by IAN WILLIAMS

ANANSI

CONTENTS

CANADIAN SHORTLIST

PREFACE

1. The poems you are about to read are

Match the poet and book in column A to the attribute in column B.

A	B
1. Billy-Ray Belcourt, *This Wound is a World*	a. At the intersection of visual design and musical orchestration.
2. Aisha Sasha John, *I have to live.*	b. Expansive, polyphonic, and socially engaged.
3. Donato Mancini, *Same Diff*	c. Unreadable. Should you read or should you look?
4. Tongo Eisen-Martin, *Heaven Is All Goodbyes*	d. Embodied, decolonializing, cerebral, and heartfelt.
5. Susan Howe, *Debths*	e. Politically and historically activated, accountable only to truth.
6. Natalie Shapero, *Hard Child*	f. Instagrammable. Earwormy. Urgent.
7. Layli Long Soldier, *Whereas*	g. The epitome of contemporary lyric beauty.

Answers: 1d, 2f, 3a, 4b, 5c, 6g, 7e

2. Mnemonic

Here's a mnemonic to help you remember the titles of this year's finalists:

This wound is a world whereas heaven is all goodbyes. Same diff. Debths. I have to live hard, child.

You can set it to a jingle if that helps.

3. Good

Most poetry books published these days are good. They have merit. They couldn't get through the publishing bouncers unless they were wearing their best sparkly outfits.

But there's how're-you-doing-I'm-good *good* and hot-dang-how'd-you-make-this-baklava *good*.

We haven't even touched *better* or *best* yet.

4. Desirables

In the business world, managers point at employees and assign *deliverables*. While reading, I had a list of *desirables*. I hoped to close a book and burst into blurb: *singular, unique, daring, brave, inventive, necessary, unprecedented, moving*. I wanted to find a book that no hyperbole could measure, a book so headslicing and heartstopping that language would give way to — to *!!!!* to emoji.

During our deliberations, Ben Lerner said, "The charisma of voice," and I swooned inside.

But sometimes the least virtuosic books were the ones that curled up inside us. They made imperceptible gestures toward poetic expectations. They were quiet, insistent books that, say, a cat would read. And some of them are on this year's list.

5. Process

It was fall 2017. I was young and naïve. I had just started reading the Griffin entries. I was determined to find something worthwhile in every book so I flagged with sticky tabs the lines that made me poetrymoan. I then shelved the books backward, with the spines facing toward the wall and the tabbed pages facing outward. That way I'd be able to tell which books had received the most hits without the encumbrance of authorship. I was also going to tweet my favourite line from every book.

As a process, this did not work. Too many books.

But it did cause me to read differently. Instead of reading toward fault (in language or reasoning), as one does a student essay, I read toward a poet's achievement and I did not stop reading until I found one. ──────

> In an earlier draft of this preface, I had an analogy about looking for raisins among bran flakes. Glad I cut it.

6. The narrow field

Two important questions emerged. One points at the self, the other outward.

Is this a book I would read again?

Is this a book I would share?

7. Competent

It is neither an insult nor a compliment when someone calls your book *competent*.

8. Consensus

Is it better for judges to reach consensus or to maintain strong preferences to the death? Is it better for the winning collection to be the one that is respectable and satisfying to most of us or the one that is polarizing, strong in its own direction, and adored by a few of us? Do you bring pastries to the potluck or baklava with potentially dangerous nuts? An economist could probably create a cost-benefit instrument for this problem.

9. Prompt 1

Assemble a poem using only poem titles from the Canadian finalists. The titles you select must come from poems in this anthology.

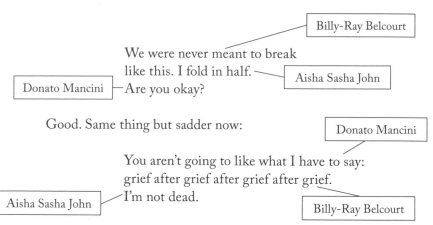

10. Trend
BTW plainspoken diction is trending. A lot of poetry is being written for quick consumption, placing little demand on the reader but still ostensibly packing emotional heat. Yeah, that kind of poetry's like super informal and caszh.

11. Prompt 2
Assemble a poem using sentences from the international finalists. Use only first or last lines.

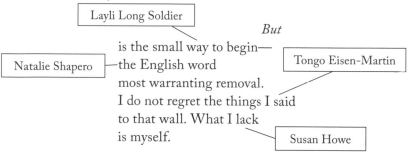

12. Friends
write books and it's hard to read these without special attention and affection. Some of these friends became your friends because of their work. Your heart has gone up and down with each poem they've placed, with the hydra of rejection they've encountered. You wish them prizes and confetti. And now that you are in a position to fulfill their dreams, can you and should you? This is a difficult question. Do they deserve it?

13. No question

Of course they do.

    Of course so many other poets do too.

14. This program is brought to you by

- The Griffin Trust: responsible for championing poetry in Canadian culture and hosting the most impressive poetry event on the calendar.
- Ruth Smith: able to coordinate like a multi-limbed Shiva, eternally cheerful, always seemingly back from walking the dog.
- Sarah Howe read hundreds of books with a months-old baby in her arms. How much poetry did her baby absorb?
- Ben Lerner: in my head, he drank coffee from the pot, slept in his glasses among the books, wore striped pyjamas.
- Me: imagine.

15. Making it

Consider the sequence of victories for poems to make it in the world. Not every line makes it into a poem, not every poem makes it past a few drafts, not every finished poem makes it into a manuscript, not every manuscript makes it past the publisher or the board. Bouncers, remember. There is so much selection along the way. Then there's the battle to get into a reader's hands. These poems have made it into yours.

In an earlier draft, I had a metaphor about millions of sperm competing against each other to fertilize an egg. It was hokey so it got cut. And at some point, we no longer think in terms of sperm and egg. The materials dissolve and the competition is forgotten and what's left is a person, you, and, in the context of the Griffin Prize, strong books.

THE GRIFFIN POETRY PRIZE
Anthology 2018

INTERNATIONAL

SHORTLIST

TONGO EISEN-MARTIN

Heaven Is All Goodbyes

Tongo Eisen-Martin's *Heaven Is All Goodbyes* moves between trenchant political critique and dreamlike association, demonstrating how, in the right hands, one mode might energize the other — keeping alternative orders of meaning alive in the face of radical injustice. Eisen-Martin's voice is a chorus of other voices, many arising from prisons and landscapes of engineered poverty; his poems are places where discourses and vernaculars collide and recombine into new configurations capable of expressing outrage and sorrow and love. This unpredictable volume is equally a work of commitment and of wonder: no false consolation, no settling for despair. Its music makes a clearing in the dominant logic of the day. "When a drummer is present, he or she is God // "I am not an I. / I am a black commons."

Faceless

A tour guide through your robbery
He also is

Cigarette saying, "look what I did about your silence."

Ransom water and box spring gold
        —This decade is only for accent grooming, I guess

Ransom water and box spring gold
        —The corner store must die

War games, I guess

All these tongues rummage junk

                The start of mass destruction
                Begins and ends
                In restaurant bathrooms
                That some people use
                And other people clean

                "you telling me there's a rag in the sky?"
                —waiting for you. yes—

we've written a scene
we've set a stage

We should have fit in. Warehouse jobs are for communists. But now more corridor and hallway have walked into our lives. Now the whistling is less playful and the barbed wire is overcrowded too.

My dear, if it is not a city, it is a prison.
If it has a prison, it is a prison. Not a city.

When a courtyard talks on behalf of military issue,
all walks take place outside of the body.

Dear life to your left
Medieval painting to your right
None of this makes an impression

Crop people living in thin air
You got five minutes
to learn how to see
through this breeze

When a mask goes sideways,
Barbed wire becomes the floor
Barbed wire becomes the roof
Forty feet into the sky
becomes out of bounds

When a mask breaks in half,
mind which way the eyes go.

They've killed the world for the sake of giving everyone the
same backstory

We're watching Gary, Indiana fight itself into the sky

Old pennies for wind. For that wind feeling you get before the
hood goes up and over your headache. Pennies that stick together
(mocking all aspirations). Stuck together pennies was the fust
newspaper I ever read. Along with the storefront dwelling army
that always lets us down.

Where the holy spirit favors the backroom. Souls in a situation
that offer one hundred ways to remain a loser. Souls watching the
clock hoping that eyes don't lie to sad people.

> *"what were we talking about again?"*
> *the narrator asked the graveyard*
> *—ten minutes flat—*
> *said the graveyard*
> *—the funeral only took ten minutes—*
> *"never tell that to anyone again,"*
> *the narrator severely replied*

"You just going to pin the 90s on me?"
—all thirty years of them—
"Then why should I know the difference between sleep and satire?"

　the pyramid of corner stores fell on our heads
　　　　—we died right away

　that building wants to climb up and jump off another building
　　　　—these are downtown decisions

somewhere on this planet, it is august 7th

and were running down the rust thinking, "one more needs to
    come with me"

                                          "What
                                          evaporated
                                          on earth, so
                                          that we could
                                          be sent back
                                          down?"

A conductor of minds
        In a city-wide symphony
        Waving souls to sing
        He also is

I have to talk to myself differently now

When a drummer is present,
They are God

"I am not an I.
I am a black commons"

I am writing out my new tattoo on bus station glass
making tattoos all afternoon
talking myself into seeing the decade through

under my skin, they call a tattoo the sky

I must really be the devil's front man

staring at an empty bus that I imagine,
in fact, carries paintings of people

and the man drunk behind the wheel
has to choose between
a black and white toddler
afterschool in america
on a california street
that doesn't need a name
nor a california

no one on the street has a job
and therefore
no one is there

"I colored my oppressor's gun
and dance floor for him in the same day,"
the joke began

"the walk under bus seats is fine by me
as long as I get to the front,"
the joke concluded

                                        and Tuesday is a
                                        rotten soup
                                        or downhill
                                        entertainment
                                        or commotion in the
                                        ashtray
                                        or the day jail quotas
                                        get filled
                                        the day that the
                                        planet plays flat

                                        Maybe the capitalist
                                        sets stadium seats
                                        on fire
                                        and calls it economic
                                        progress

The communist has plenty of time
To finish his cigarette
and lie to his boss

A killer lying down in front of a tank
I have a small statue built in my chest
and also, an anchor upside down in the air

worried about the walls
I forgot the ceiling was closing in on me too
—my take on my alcoholism

I am hunched over a meal
I ate five years ago
—my take on the look on my face

                                He cursed God a little
                    then took another step up the staircase

        and for a second, forgot all occupants of the world
                                beginning with this house

he (this action hero of one street proportions) declared:

"rap music is the way I count blessings. The '80s were better
than its fiction. I got a piece of fence meshed through my skull.
I will be half-eaten my entire life. Always walking beside myself
with a gun to my head and another one pointed at passers by.
And it's half of me or all of you. Walking in and out of myself.
But I'm always happy to see you, brother. What a miraculous
route you took through the threat!"

honest pay
is a knife in his arm

honest pay in my chest
is a broken lock on the monument

tell you the truth
I forget what his hands looked like
What he did with them
What kind of third eye the cuffs cut into his wrist

Heaven Is All Goodbyes

A 1978 statement

My brother Biko and I are driving
In an empty cell lane

We are God's evil to these settlers
They might throw us under the shift change

We take wolf naps

We don't know what else we good at besides this traveling

State lines in a night tide passing through beachhead america
Passing with hurricane memory
—Three thousand exits of sludge-bathed apartheid

Everything south of canada is extrajudicial gun oil
And your local unemployment factory

In a few hours we will fit in   Relax for now

Hop out of the car and I'm a dirty shoe illusion
Leaning on the trunk with the ghosts of switchblades
                                        And other rusty services

I am enemy humor
And traveling

Father's ashes on the back seat behind two sons

                              In a lane not for metaphor
                Well, maybe a metaphor about something unfinished
                —One million hands passing us through the Midwest

Last wishes by way of fishtail / Day dreams by way of collision /
    Home in the badlands of translation / Relaxed passing / Great
    grandparents' finger bones / Father's ashes / No longer arms /
    Just tattoos

Badlands imagination
Barreling
Translating
A father's last trip home

We don't know what else we good at besides this traveling

Exits in collage / Exits in pieces / Pieces of 1970s kitchen plates /
    In a good luck refrigerator / We still ain't ate / The narcotic
    swing of how we see yesterday

Get out of the car against desperate white supremacy

Gas station greetings
Stray dogs
And other earth-born alarms
        We are stray deadly

Against desperate white supremacy / And other senses /
    That die silly / And have murdered

We don't know what else we good at
Besides this traveling

Two coins / or the toll is us

Character interstate on a journey of a million parallels

Some like us better high / Some like us better drunk / Every late
    night has a summer to it / Cousin breeze and murder rate

Barreling like gut born love songs
Your ancestors are smiling
As we pass the time
When we ride
It's language

Passed Gary 3000
Cast iron lining / Proud forearms for meals

Three-man ghost story

Fishers of ourselves

Cards dealt

Narrative implied

Maybe something unfinished

Like an Indiana hurricane
Or two midnights in Milwaukee

Or no arms
No tattoos
No Chicago
Ever again

We don't know what else we good at
Besides this traveling

And besides
Heaven is all goodbyes
Anyway

Three buildings make a tide

I do not regret the things I said to that wall
stories about hand ratios in brawls
and a hotel kitchen entrance killer
and steamboats where they dedicate their one-night stand to
    driftwood
                    While we look at all the pretty kingdoms floating
                        over our tents
                                    While we get the surplus treatment

Don't put your shoe on my shoulder
And call it a hand (one building makes a jail)

"that's a lot of people for
only a little bit of commotion"

                                    The bookshelf looks alive to me
                    Alive and my opposition (until the devil lets me go)

                                    My sidekick is the bootlegger

I tied up our friend as soon as a couple rich people acted like they
                                    cared about him

                    A painting of a sun watched me end lives

The point I was making began scaring other patrons in the pool hall

"who would name themselves after this city?"
—to which I reply, "the only woman for me."

Calling my drug the scoundrel and cousin / an axe handle in its
    five minutes as a twin

Painting my walls with pieces of other walls

                I wandered to the edge of the parking lot

SUSAN HOWE

Debths

In a 2014 lecture, Susan Howe quoted Robert Duncan on how poetry's secret lies in the "keeping of time": "Counting the measures . . . one image may recall another, finding depth in the resounding." It's an apt description of Howe's own method in her extraordinary new book, *Debths*, which continues to plumb the intertextual depths (also at once *debts* and *deaths*) of the archives and collections that have fed her work for almost thirty years. Across the book's four sections, we hear its poems resound in sympathy not only with their reinvented source materials, but with earlier moments in Howe's career — one of the most significant, innovative, and humane in recent American letters — whose varied threads this new work draws triumphantly together. As Howe writes in her evocative foreword, "Secret connections among artifacts are audible and visible and yet hidden until you take a leap. . . . It's the mystery of strong music in the soul." The strong music of *Debths* reveals itself in poems to be returned to again and again with growing astonishment and gratitude.

Epistolary Correspondences. *From the foreword*

Before I was sent to Little Sir Echo I had an imaginary friend who lived in our Buffalo mailbox. His name was Mr. Bickle. When we moved to Cambridge he vanished as transitional objects tend to do although his name lives on as a family anecdote.

Strange that one half-suffocated picnic in the course of life can disappear into Lake Armington's hanging rock echo portals. Until the replication of love prevails in art and "Periscope" one of Paul Thek's late "picture-light" paintings bubbles up from puddle blue depths

So many things happen by bringing to light what has long been hidden in this psychic acousmatic toiling moil. Betwixt and between. Between what? Oh everything. Take your microphone. Cross your voice with the ocean.

I'm here. I'm still American.

from **Titian Air Vent**

Te turo turo

Running footsteps. Interlete te interlute. Ages have passed.
A bell of the Chou Dynasty is in my hands. Goodbye for
the present. I seem to go back to things that do not belong
to me. Call when you get depressed. There are those of us
at a distance who may have seemed to drop out of touch but
never really did

For what Porpoise

My body is made of bones. In times of trouble and perplexity I
can bend my limbs and stretch half fish half Fishman in
Excelsis. A luminous aura surrounds all things numenonal.
No need for money money money

  Believe me I am not rubbish

"they are crowded with o·
and reworkings" crowde(
little monuments of paint
inch a space of scrutiny ar
Scattered marks and loop
off words from images twi
from their original source
history scattered to the fou
of a page it was *you* playin,
There are those of us who ɪ
ᴜⅼᴏ ᴀᴜⅴⅼⅴᴏ ᴄᴆⅼⅼⅼⅼⅼᴕⅰⅼ ᴏᴜᴄ̄
Oh the grows, leaf sown
^

was   dread   ~~has is~~
~~s~~ing what ~~is~~ lost & ~~hate~~ what is won
ɹdistinct, yet stirring and working
ctive faculty partook of DEATH, and
into which the sap was yet to be
d of smoke to me by day, yet they
uring my wanderings through the
out crossing, the sandy deserts of
ng converted into an irreligious
⋯ ⋯ ⋯ ⋯ be an instance. But
That tremble in the stream below—

er's edges. The par-
n underneath, half
:hance for any unity
d, dust and puddle,
'pposition in its most
, and yet all will be
ITTLE above eye-
d if not a little below

from **Periscope**

Closed book who stole

who away do brackets

signify emptiness was

it a rift in experience

Mackeral and porpoise

was this the last of us

These tallied scraps float

like glass skiffs quietly for

love or pity and all that

What an idea in such a time

as ours Pip among Pleiads

If to sense you are

alive is pleasant itself

or can be nearly so—

If I know what it is

I'll show it—but no

What I lack is myself

from **Debths**

ŏ mў Soul ᵗʰᵗ ᵇⁱᵗ and Rătūrn ˣᶠ ᴹ˟ᴵ˗

[?Whv/?Which] the had lack
←—quality:—→

32

```
078 Nothing        1141 Nothing 4      1160 Nothing 5
078 Nothing        1147 Nothing 5      1175 Diarmuid 1
082 Nothing        1148 Nothing 5      1180 Diarmuid 1
082 Nothing        1148 Nothing 5      1181 Diarmuid 1
083 Nothing        1152 Nothing 5      1184 Diarmuid 1
103 Nothing        1153 Nothing 5      1184 Diarmuid 1
104 Nothing        1154 Nothing 5      1187 Diarmuid 1
104 Nothing        1160 Nothing 5      1189 Diarmuid 2
111 Nothing        1160 Nothing 5
111 Nothing
112 Nothing
113 Nothing
119 Nothing 3
126 Nothing 4
```

NATALIE SHAPERO

Hard Child

The poems in Natalie Shapero's *Hard Child* come as close as lyric poems can to perfection. We feel the effect of them before noticing their machinery. Yet every poetic instinct Shapero possesses, every decision of line, image, stanza, diction, and tone, results in poems that are limber, athletic, powerful, and balanced. And behind her technical choices lies an emerging ethics: "I don't want any more of what I have. / I don't want another spider plant. I don't // want another lover." Her poems take us to the purest evolutionary point of the lyric form through their single-speaker stance, the movement of a mind over subjects, the emotional weight carried on the backs of images, the unpredictable associations, the satisfying callbacks. She teaches us how to retain the self without disappearing into the object we behold. She holds herself at various distances from the thing considered. She drives us toward a view and back again. This is how to write a lyric poem.

My Hand and Cold

Of surgeons putting their knives to erroneous

body parts, stories abound. So can you really blame
my neighbor for how, heading into the operation,
he wrote across his good knee NOT THIS KNEE?

The death of me: I'm never half so bold. *You will
feel*, the doctor said, *my hand and cold*—

and I thought of the pub quiz question: Which three
countries are entirely inside of other countries?
I bought the bound ONE THOUSAND NAMES
FOR BABY, made two lists: one if she's born breathing,

one if not. The second list was longer. So much

that I might call her, if she were never to bear
the name, never turn to it, suffer shaming, mull its
range and implications, blame it, change it, move

away to San Marino, Vatican City, Lesotho.

Hard Child

So I had two lists of names for a girl, so
what. The president's allowed to
have two speeches, in case the hostage
comes home in a bag. The geese
in the metropark don't want
for bread crumbs, despite the signs
proclaiming the land provides them all
they need. I was a hard child, by which
I mean I was callous from the start.
Even now, were I to find myself, after
a grand disease or blast, among the pasty
scattering of survivors, there isn't one
human tradition I would choose to carry
forward. Not marking feast days, not
assembling roadside shrines, not marrying
up, not researching the colloquialism
STATEN ISLAND DIVORCE, not
representing paste pearls as the real
things, not recounting how the advent
of photography altered painting,
soured us on the acrylic portrait, thrust us
toward the abstract, sent us seeking
to capture in oil that which film would
never be wasted on: umbrella stands,
unlovely grates, assorted drains, body casts.
I typically hate discussing the past
and treasure the option, rarer and rarer,
to turn from it, as when K.'s twins
were born and one of them
nearly died—I don't even remember which,
that's how much they got better.

You Look Like I Feel

Dirt on my chin and I wonder: Am I already
in the ground? Like a toy turned real, I cannot shed
the sense that I have died. The German word

for heaven's the same

as the German word for sky. On hearing a cruel
prince was in danger, I prayed for him to thrive,
not for his own sake, but for the concubines,

sure to end up buried

along. To my real face, a man once crowed
I RUINED YOU, and though he did, the joke's
on him: he ruined me only for this world,

and this world is not long

for itself. The earth, that ever-loving
but distrustful kin, keeps leaving us just a little
pocket money when it dies, never the land—

Old Ad

The English word most warranting removal
from our language is UNBEARABLE;

all I see is people keeping on.

Scrubbing the kitchen, she told me she had three
hearts. One was charged

with delivering blood throughout the dim
aquarium of her body, one was dead
along with her mother, and one persisted
to grieve on behalf of the world.

The Kennedys lost a baby while in office.

I swear to God I hardly think of the past.

Even the old ad doesn't quite make mention
of the great terror we're ordered to remember:

DRINK COCA-COLA. NOW IN OVER THIRTY-FIVE
ALLIED AND NEUTRAL NATIONS.

Teacup This

To my young daughter, I sing the songs

my mother sang to me. Which is to say: to my young daughter,
I sing an eclectic selection of breakup tunes of the '60s and '70s.
*Now I know you're not the only starfish in the sea / If I never hear your
name again, it's all the same to me* … That doesn't seem quite right

to sing to a baby, yet here I am. And here she is: bed-sprawled,
unblessed, and so perhaps like the starfish, yes—one creature of
more

than the world requires, as I am unceasingly reminded
by pamphlet mandates, blanket labels, alerts to lay her always up.
It's awful, to be a person. That's why, from my lovers, I've always
demanded

to know what kind of a dog I might be, were I ever a dog, and don't
say teacup this, toy that, don't pick a dog that must travel all over
stuffed in a bag like a filthy magazine. Don't take it lightly
when I say of all the men I've been with, there are only a few

I never would allow to hold my child. I consider
this a triumph.

Passing and Violence

What pride I feel in America stems from our anthem
being the toughest one to sing. The high segment
with the red burn of the rocket: only a few
can reach. Watching a stranger parallel park, I pray
she abrades her neighbor. Watching football, I need
to see a man die. I need to see the intractable passing

and violence. Of the cruelty ringing the earth,
I am a portion. I never said he was *a bad man*, only
a larger portion. He wreaked harm on us for years
and then one day he began to die. I watched as science
shattered his body to wrest the disease out, stopping
just short of his failure. *Failure*, the word
he favored over death. Me, I favored nothing over
death. I held him like a brother. I knew him as an error
of God, dropped at the doorstep of our age, and what
could we do but save him? I began to suspect so many
of machinations. How my parents had summoned me
into this world, but then when I arrived,

they were not here. My whole being was a setup.
They called me over to sit alone with the weather
and soot, unfettered. They said I had differences to be
resolved. After attempting the anthem, upward of fifty
percent remark, *I should have started lower* or *I should
have chosen something else instead*. Uneasy lies the head.

Ten What

The camera adds ten what, I can't remember.
But the threat's enough to make me stay

away. I don't want any more of what I have.
I don't want another spider plant. I don't

want another lover. Especially I don't want
another clock, except insofar as each of us

is a clock, all hammers and counting
down. And yes, I know by heart the list

of lifetimes. A worker bee will die before
a camel. A fox will die before a pilot whale.

A pocket watch will die before the clock inside
the crocodile—I think of this often, but never

tell my lover, as I do not tell him that,
upstairs, a moth is pinned by the window

sash. I make no plans to free it. Everyone says
the baby looks like me, but I can't see it.

LAYLI LONG SOLDIER

Whereas

Layli Long Soldier's *Whereas* repurposes congressional doublespeak in order to lay bare the murderous hypocrisy lurking behind the official language of the state. Deftly deploying a variety of techniques and idioms, Long Soldier has crafted an intricate and urgent counter-history, a work of elegy, outrage, and profound generosity that explores what possibilities of interconnection in the present might be enabled by a genuine reckoning with the past. "I am a citizen of the United States and an enrolled member of the Oglala Sioux Tribe," Long Soldier writes in the introduction to the title poem, "meaning I am a citizen of the Oglala Lakota Nation — and in this dual citizenship, I must work, I must eat, I must art, I must mother, I must friend, I must listen, I must observe, constantly I must live."

from **Ȟe Sápa**

Three

This is how you see me the space in which to place me

The space in me you see

This is how to place you in the space in which to see

is this place

see how you place me in you · To see this space

47

Four

But
is the small way to begin.

But I could not.

As I am limited to few
words at command, such as *waŋblí.*   This
was how I wanted to begin, with the little
I know.

But could not.

Because this waŋblí, this eagle
of my imagining is not spotted, bald,
nor even a nest-eagle. It is gold,
though by definition, not ever the great Golden Eagle.
Much as the gold, by no mistake, is not ground-gold,
man-gold or nugget.   But here, it is
the gold of   light and wing   together.
Wings that do not close, but   in expanse
angle up so slightly; plunge with muscle
and stout head somewhere between
my uncle, son, father, brother.

But I failed   to begin there, with this
expanse.   Much as I failed to start
with the great point in question.
There in muscle in high inner flight always
in the plunge we fear for the falling, we buckle to wonder:
What man is expendable?

from **Vaporative**

.

Strange how lying on this side works
yet on my back I grieve and turning
to my left I rewind to a child's world
so I re-turn back over to the first
position of poesis prenascent page
before any material thing makes
in this right-side peace I work most
nights I greet open-eyed delicate
pronunciations like *thank you* I thank
the empty room I still my body I work hard
not to slip a centimeter in dark work not to
interrupt my own conversation I move
my mouth as if silently reading as if a begin
ner or courting a friendship careful holding
to my chest small gifts tight 3-lettered
words in 3-word phrases I welcome in
the new new.

38

Here, the sentence will be respected.

I will compose each sentence with care, by minding what the rules of writing dictate.

For example, all sentences will begin with capital letters.

Likewise, the history of the sentence will be honored by ending each one with appropriate punctuation such as a period or question mark, thus bringing the idea to (momentary) completion.

You may like to know, I do not consider this a "creative piece."

I do not regard this as a poem of great imagination or a work of fiction.

Also, historical events will not be dramatized for an "interesting" read.

Therefore, I feel most responsible to the orderly sentence; conveyor of thought.

That said, I will begin.

You may or may not have heard about the Dakota 38.

If this is the first time you've heard of it, you might wonder, "What is the Dakota 38?"

The Dakota 38 refers to thirty-eight Dakota men who were executed by hanging, under orders from President Abraham Lincoln.

To date, this is the largest "legal" mass execution in US history.

The hanging took place on December 26, 1862—the day after Christmas.

This was the *same week* that President Lincoln signed the Emancipation Proclamation.

In the preceding sentence, I italicize "same week" for emphasis.

There was a movie titled *Lincoln* about the presidency of Abraham Lincoln.

The signing of the Emancipation Proclamation was included in the film *Lincoln*; the hanging of the Dakota 38 was not.

In any case, you might be asking, "Why were thirty-eight Dakota men hung?"

As a side note, the past tense of hang is *hung*, but when referring to the capital punishment of hanging, the correct past tense is *hanged*.

So it's possible that you're asking, "Why were thirty-eight Dakota men hanged?"

They were hanged for the Sioux Uprising.

I want to tell you about the Sioux Uprising, but I don't know where to begin.

I may jump around and details will not unfold in chronological order.

Keep in mind, I am not a historian.

So I will recount facts as best as I can, given limited resources and understanding.

Before Minnesota was a state, the Minnesota region, generally speaking, was the traditional homeland for Dakota, Anishinaabeg, and Ho-Chunk people.

During the 1800s, when the US expanded territory, they "purchased" land from the Dakota people as well as the other tribes.

But another way to understand that sort of "purchase" is: Dakota leaders ceded land to the US government in exchange for money or goods, but most importantly, the safety of their people.

Some say that Dakota leaders did not understand the terms they were entering, or they never would have agreed.

Even others call the entire negotiation "trickery."

But to make whatever-it-was official and binding, the US government drew up an initial treaty.

This treaty was later replaced by another (more convenient) treaty, and then another.

I've had difficulty unraveling the terms of these treaties, given the legal speak and congressional language.

As treaties were abrogated (broken) and new treaties were drafted, one after another, the new treaties often referenced old defunct treaties, and it is a muddy, switchback trail to follow.

Although I often feel lost on this trail, I know I am not alone.

However, as best as I can put the facts together, in 1851, Dakota territory was contained to a twelve-mile by one-hundred-fifty-mile long strip along the Minnesota River.

But just seven years later, in 1858, the northern portion was ceded (taken) and the southern portion was (conveniently) allotted, which reduced Dakota land to a stark ten-mile tract.

These amended and broken treaties are often referred to as the Minnesota Treaties.

The word *Minnesota* comes from *mni*, which means water; and *sota*, which means turbid.

Synonyms for turbid include muddy, unclear, cloudy, confused, and smoky.

Everything is in the language we use.

For example, a treaty is, essentially, a contract between two sovereign nations.

The US treaties with the Dakota Nation were legal contracts that promised money.

It could be said, this money was payment for the land the Dakota ceded; for living within assigned boundaries (a reservation); and for relinquishing rights to their vast hunting territory which, in turn, made Dakota people dependent on other means to survive: money.

The previous sentence is circular, akin to so many aspects of history.

As you may have guessed by now, the money promised in the turbid treaties did not make it into the hands of Dakota people.

In addition, local government traders would not offer credit to "Indians" to purchase food or goods.

Without money, store credit, or rights to hunt beyond their ten-mile tract of land, Dakota people began to starve.

The Dakota people were starving.

The Dakota people starved.

In the preceding sentence, the word "starved" does not need italics for emphasis.

One should read "The Dakota people starved" as a straightforward and plainly stated fact.

As a result—and without other options but to continue to starve—Dakota people retaliated.

Dakota warriors organized, struck out, and killed settlers and traders.

This revolt is called the Sioux Uprising.

Eventually, the US Cavalry came to Mnisota to confront the Uprising.

More than one thousand Dakota people were sent to prison.

As already mentioned, thirty-eight Dakota men were subsequently hanged.

After the hanging, those one thousand Dakota prisoners were released.

However, as further consequence, what remained of Dakota territory in Mnisota was dissolved (stolen).

The Dakota people had no land to return to.

This means they were exiled.

Homeless, the Dakota people of Mnisota were relocated (forced) onto reservations in South Dakota and Nebraska.

Now, every year, a group called the Dakota 38 + 2 Riders conduct a memorial horse ride from Lower Brule, South Dakota, to Mankato, Mnisota.

The Memorial Riders travel 325 miles on horseback for eighteen days, sometimes through sub-zero blizzards.

They conclude their journey on December 26, the day of the hanging.

Memorials help focus our memory on particular people or events.

Often, memorials come in the forms of plaques, statues, or gravestones.

The memorial for the Dakota 38 is not an object inscribed with words, but an *act*.

Yet, I started this piece because I was interested in writing about grasses.

So, there is one other event to include, although it's not in chronological order and we must backtrack a little.

When the Dakota people were starving, as you may remember, government traders would not extend store credit to "Indians."

One trader named Andrew Myrick is famous for his refusal to provide credit to Dakota people by saying, "If they are hungry, let them eat grass."

There are variations of Myrick's words, but they are all something to that effect.

When settlers and traders were killed during the Sioux Uprising, one of the first to be executed by the Dakota was Andrew Myrick.

When Myrick's body was found,

$\qquad\qquad\qquad\qquad\qquad$ his mouth was stuffed with grass.

I am inclined to call this act by the Dakota warriors a poem.

There's irony in their poem.

There was no text.

"Real" poems do not "really" require words.

I have italicized the previous sentence to indicate inner dialogue, a revealing moment.

But, on second thought, the words "Let them eat grass" click the gears of the poem into place.

So, we could also say, language and word choice are crucial to the poem's work.

Things are circling back again.

Sometimes, when in a circle, if I wish to exit, I must leap.

And let the body   swing.

From the platform.

                        Out

                                    to the grasses.

from **Whereas Statements**

WHEREAS the word *whereas* means it being the case that, or considering that, or while on the contrary; is a qualifying or introductory statement, a conjunction, a connector. Whereas sets the table. The cloth. The saltshakers and plates. Whereas calls me to the table. Whereas precedes and invites. I have come now. I'm seated across from a Whereas smile. Under pressure of formalities, I fidget I shake my legs. I'm not one for these smiles, Whereas I have spent my life in unholding. *What do you mean by unholding?* Whereas asks and since Whereas rarely asks, I am moved to respond, Whereas, I have learned to exist and exist without your formality, saltshakers, plates, cloth. Without the slightest conjunctions to connect me. Without an exchange of questions, without the courtesy of answers. It is mine, this unholding, so that with or without the setup, I can see the dish being served. Whereas let us bow our heads in prayer now, just enough to eat;

CANADIAN

SHORTLIST

BILLY-RAY BELCOURT

This Wound is a World

Blending the resources of love song and elegy, prayer and manifesto, Billy-Ray Belcourt's *This Wound is a World* shows us poetry at its most intimate and politically necessary. Mindful of tangled lineages and the lingering erasures of settler colonialism, Belcourt crafts poems in which "history lays itself bare" — but only as bare as their speaker's shape-shifting heart. Belcourt pursues original forms with which to chart the constellations of queerness and indigeneity, rebellion and survival, desire and embodiedness these poems so fearlessly explore. Between its bold treatment of sexuality and wary anatomy of despair, *This Wound is a World* peels back the layers of feeling and experience to offer, finally, the glimmerings of hope — which only sometimes looks like escape: "follow me out the backdoor of the world." This electrifying book reminds us that a poem may live twin lives as incantation and inscription, singing from the untamed margins: "grieve is the name i give to myself / i carve it into the bed frame. / i am make-believe. / this is an archive. / it hurts to be a story."

Gay Incantations

i fall into the opening between subject and object
and call it a condition of possibility.
when i speak only the ceiling listens.
sometimes it moans.
if i have a name,
let it be the sound his lips make.
there is no word in my language for this.
sometimes my kookum begins to cry
and a world falls out.
grieve is the name i give to myself.
i carve it into the bed frame.
i am make-believe.
this is an archive.
it hurts to be a story.
i am the boundary between reality and fiction.
it is a ghost town.
you dreamt me out of existence.
you are at once a map to nowhere and everywhere.
yesterday was an optical illusion.
i kiss a stranger and give him a middle name.
i call this love.
it lasts for exactly twenty minutes.
i chase after that feeling.
which is to say:
i want to almost not exist.
almost is the closest i can get to the sky.
heaven is a wormhole.
i first found it in another man's armpit.
last night i gave birth to a woman and named her becoming.
she is four cree girls between the ages of 10 and 14 from northern
saskatchewan.
we are a home movie
i threw out by accident.
all that is left is the signified.
people die that way.

The Rez Sisters II

after tomson highway

cast:

girl of surplus. girl who is made from fragments. she who can only
be spoken of by way of synecdoche. she whose name cannot be
enunciated only mouthed.

mother of that which cannot be mothered. mother who wants
nothing and everything at the same time. she who gave birth to
herself three times: 1. the miscarriage. 2. the shrunken world.
3. the aftermath.

sister of forest fire. sister who dwells in the wreckage. she who
forages for the right things in the wrong places. nothing is utopia
and so she prays to a god for a back that can bend like a tree
splitting open to make room for the heat.

aunt of the sovereignty of dust. aunt of that which cannot be
negated entirely. she who is magic because she goes missing and
comes back. she who walks upside down on the ceiling of the
world and does not fall.

kookum of love in spite of it all. kookum who made a man out of
a memory. she who is a country unto herself.

father of ash. father of a past without a mouth. he who ate too much
of the sunset.

We Were Never Meant to Break Like This

1. follow me out of the backdoor of the world.

2. how do you tell someone that they are helping you stay tuned into life?

3. what does it mean that her first breath was also her last?

4. i am so sad that i burrow into the absence of every boy who has held me.

5. i kiss him knowing that when i wake up i will be in a body differently.

6. the future is already over, but that doesn't mean we don't have anywhere else to go.

Grief After Grief After Grief After Grief

1. my body is a stray bullet. i was made from crossfire. love was her last resort. his mouth, a revolver. i come from four hundred no man's lands.

2. "smell my armpit again / i miss it when you do that."[1]

3. his moaning is an honour song i want to world to.

4. one of the conditions of native life today is survivor's guilt.

5. it is july 2016 and the creator opens up the sky to attend a #blacklivesmatter protest. there, she bumps into *weesageechak* and warns him that if policemen don't stop killing black men she will flood america and it will become a lost country only grieving mothers will know how to find. this, she says, is how the world will end and be rebuilt this time.

6. haunting is a gender. gender is another word for horror story.

7. "i can hear him screaming for me, and i can hear him saying, 'stop, honey help me.'"[2]

8. i am trying to figure out how to be in the world without wanting it. this, perhaps, is what it means to be native.

---

[1] from *Lilting* (2014, dir. Hong Khaou).
[2] see: http://www.cbc.ca/news/canada/calgary/rcmp-gleichen-christian-duck-chief-excessive-force-1.3521620.

from **The Oxford Journal**

II.

how does it feel to be an object? you wear your favorite pair of
ripped jeans exposing your brown flesh to the world. this
exposure is interpreted as an invitation, compelling a stranger in
a centuries-old building to walk up to you, rub your skin, laugh,
and walk away. you laugh too, but only because your body needs
to escape itself, to identify something of an ontological rupture.
this is what it feels like to almost not exist. you keep surviving
anyway.

VI.

you are called "wonderfully exotic." a man looks at you, tilts his
head, and presses that you are "too mixed" for him to pinpoint
any sort of ethnic belonging. this is a world-threatening feeling:
to be so other that you barely exist in a place whose imperial
conquests sought the destruction of your people. when you tell
him you are native he doesn't say anything. he lets the silence do
the talking, as if he were lamenting the violence that went into
producing someone like you. i can tell he has heard a thing or
two about us. "i have never met a native american before," he
adds, quieter this time. perhaps speaking in a hushed voice
makes you less real. what does one do with the sense of loss that
tailgates their body?

VIII.

you and a friend are going for coffee after a lecture on marxist feminist theory and a white british man nudges you with his shoulder. your friend goes to grab a table, a table that he was also intending to grab. he gets visibly upset and, willfully and passionately, says *i'm just trying to get away from you people.* your friend is stunned and in the meantime he returns to say something else under his breath. at this point, you confront him and tell him that he is out of line even though you know that the world is his to claim. he walks away, but throws more words at you. the violence of *you people* is that it is a classic interpellative call, one that pulls you outside yourself, that seeks to trap you in a flattened form of subjectivity. for him, we were nothing. this is the ebb and flow of everyday life in oxford.

AISHA SASHA JOHN

I have to live.

Aisha Sasha John's *I have to live.* shows what poetry can become when stripped of prettiness and polite convention — when in survival mode. Spontaneous, its subjects unposed, its language unrehearsed, each poem has the effect of being taken with a Polaroid camera. John writes poems that are resistant to overwrought aesthetics, poems that have popular appeal yet are uninhibited by audience, poems whose casual demeanour belies their fight against casualty. They wind their way into us like a chorus. They gain force by accumulation: "I do. / I did it. / I did. / I had to. / I have to. / I have to live." As a result, one does not engage with *I have to live.* by familiar means of dissection and analysis. One need only listen, as to an aching friend. No need to fix anything. Just listen.

I like it when we give the world to itself

Folding it to it
Like a soft-shelled taco. Hi, God.

I said in the photo's caption.
It's Aisha.

I volunteer.

I do.
I did it.
I did.
I had to.
I have to.
I have to live.

I can't believe I agreed to go to work today.

That was so dumb of me.
I hate money.
And I hate sitting down.

I fold in half

Documents destined for the shredder.

I leave flat the ones to be scanned into patient charts.

I consider how long stickers have rested on the glass
Protecting me from potential
Disease and violence
Of the people.

The first time I came here I was late, I was scolded
I was bleeding.
I barely even cared
Fuck, look:
When I start to bleed
I have to eat.

He thinks I should be glad because they

Like the idea of Aisha. I am not the idea of Aisha.

I am Aisha.

You I know you

Love the idea of Aisha.

I am not the idea of Aisha.

I am not the idea of Aisha.

I am Aisha.

I was born and I lived

Swishing fluoride around my mouth with the others.
From various classmates, I stole
Blue scissors, a hamburger sharpener, ten bucks.
My mom found the ten bucks.
She beat me.
I'm sorry
The teacher told me to say to Mandeep.
So I said, crying, I'm sorry, Mandeep.

The landlord said he lost his phone.

The tenant she said call it.
He said I did, I did
And then the tenant's boyfriend was like
I called you and a girl picked up and
Said it was the wrong number.
(And I'm like okay so it was the wrong number why are you even
Telling the guy that)
And then her boyfriend was like ya, I called it four times
She said it was the wrong number.
And then, then I was like okay. Hmm what the fuck.
And the tenant was like maybe it was your wife?
And her boyfriend was like no it
Was a girl.
So there's a
Question there.

Also apparently the dog likes the cat
But the cat
Does not like the dog.

The goat

He has to bray.
To pull his rope leash in the light.
He did it again in the black-blue sky
Of my leaving.
It is death.
He has to fucking bray
Because he is alive
And
Tied up.

I asked Fadwa what
A phrase meant;
It had hooked my bad ear and what
She said is it meant
You should be
Shy.

And then Manuela said my buns were horns
Were my tied-up
Sex.
I released them.
Je ne sais pas how to say this en anglais mais
My selves:
I suppose we
Gave me a course
Making our soul of a fitness enough
To scorn you
But not enough to
Not scorn you –
D'accord?

I'm not dead.

A person named "Jonathan Valelly" asked me to
Do something I did not want to
Do and so I did not do
It
Because I don't care (it is cold outside)
(I have snot in my nose) plus I
Don't give a
Fuck.

An oval on my pant leg of oil.

The world its lips
Get on me.

The sweet and cold
Wet of the world.

Lay it down
By Al Green featuring someone else.

I don't want no-
Body else,

He sings
Lay it down.

Let it go.
Fall in love, he says/sings.

Of things evil as well as good
Long intercourse

Induces love.

DONATO MANCINI

Same Diff

Donato Mancini's *Same Diff* crosses pre-existing texts with a strong design impulse to assemble a work of unusual beauty, resonance, and timelessness. In "Snowline," a famous French phrase about snow is translated over centuries; translations snow down the pages until the original phrase is buried; they fall through different hands until they turn from snow into a meditation on time. Mancini's primary methods are curatorial (he assembles), orchestral (he co-ordinates), mechanical (he repeats), and archaeological (he excavates language rather than the world for his materials). He fractures words to let out their yolk. *Same Diff* is a monument to Mancini's accomplishments: he uses the words of others without appropriation; he negotiates self-effacement, humility, and invisibility; he offers a way to recover a self, not through self-assertion but by attending to the voices and needs of others. What belongs to any of us? Even Mancini's words never seem to be his. He is a custodian of language who returns it to us cleaned.

RU
OK

before i start i want to say you shouldn't blame yourself
there's no point in beating around the bush
there's something we need to talk about
this is the most difficult thing i've ever had to tell
    anyone
the longer i wait the harder it's going to be
it's best if we face this right now
what i'm about to tell you won't be easy to hear
i know this will hurt but it has to be said
i don't like being the bearer of bad news
please sit down, this could come as a shock
you knew this was coming, right?
i hope this won't be a complete surprise
hate to break it to you
please don't kill the messenger
i have some really bad news
how do i even say this
this is really really hard for me
there are no words for what i have to tell you
i can't go on lying anymore
you aren't going to like what i have to say

from **Snowline**

> "*Forty days of snow are
> registered in the Paris archives
> of 1435, the trees died and the
> birds . . .*"

Mais où sont les neiges d'antan? (1461 François Villon)

But where is the last yeares snow? (1653)

Tell me, if ye know; What is come of last year's snow? (1835)

Where is fled the south wind's snow? (1835)

But where are the snows of yester-year? (1869)

But where is the last year's snow? (1877)

Where are the Snows of Yesterday? (1902)

But where are the winter's snows? (1905)

But where are the last year's snows? (1914)

Where are the snows that fell last year? (1917)

But where are the snows of last year gone? (1968)

But where are last year's snows? (1968)

But where shall last year's snow be found? (1969)

Where, Mother of God, is last year's snow? (1973)

O where are gone the snows of yore? (2013)

But where do they sleep, the snows of last year? (2014)

where goes snow when snow goes? (2014)

from **Where do you feel?**

in my eyes

in my face

in my voice

in my neck

in my throat

in my shoulders

in my heart

in my lungs

in my whole bloody body

in my social organs in general

in everywhere, flushing, sweating, pounding heart

in my collarbone and neck area

in my hands, tingling or prickling sensations

in my left shoulder blade, aches and pounds

in my stomach, and my back is paining too

in my arms, my arms feel big and heavy

in my stomach i feel tense, i feel like i am losing out,
i become immobilized on things because i can't make up my
mind on anything

in my throat there's a huge lump and i feel as if i'm
drowning, my husband says the light goes out in my eyes and
my eyes look dead

in my chest i feel a heaviness, and i feel like there is a
brick at the back of my neck, my back begins aching, whole
body feels tense

in my entire body, it aches and feels like it's going to
break, slow, heavy, lethargic, and painful, every morning
i wake with a sore throat, headache, and blocked nose

in my head i feel pressures, and tension in the back of
my neck, pain in my limbs, and frequent headaches, parts
of my body feel as if they don't belong to me

in my skin and muscles, a leaden heaviness,
constant exhaustion, and a sense of restriction and
tightening – the bare materiality of my body, sometimes
a literal freezing and reification, I'm incapable of
resonating with my environment

in my head, like it's stuffed full of lead, lethargic, my
legs feel heavy all the time and i feel ridiculously tired,
sometimes i feel so numb i feel like i can't eat anything or
i feel too sad to eat

in my chest, very tight, often the emotional and mental pain
is so severe it's very nearly a physical pain, i feel as
though i literally have a broken heart, massive exhaustion,
where my body won't co-operate, as though i'd been very
physically active for a long period and needed to rest

in my chest, the tip of this huge upside-down stony pyramid
weighs right down on top of my chest, the tip is rounded or
flat, it's just higher than my heart to the right a little,
maybe this is mostly anxiety, right there in the air, i try
to swipe it away with my hand, i try not to fall back from
the weight pushing

or
more
more or less
more more or or less less
more more more more or or or less less
more more more more more or or or or less less less
more more more more more more more or or or or or less less less
more more more more more more more more or or or or or or less less less less
more more more more more more more or or or or or less less less
more more more more more or or or or less less less
more more more more or or or less less
more more or or less less
more or less
more
or
or
or less more
or or less less more more
or or or or less less less more more
or or or or or less less less less more more more
or or or or or or or less less less less less more more more
or or or or or or or or less less less less less less more more more more
or or or or or or or less less less less less more more more
or or or or or less less less less more more more
or or or or less less less more more
or or less less more more
or less more
or
less
less
less more or
less less more more or or
less less less less more more more or or
less less less less less more more more more or or or
less less less less less less less more more more more more or or or
less less less less less less less less more more more more more more or or or or
less less less less less less less more more more more more or or or
less less less less less more more more more or or or
less less less less more more more or or
less less more more or or
less more or
less
or

Notes for "Snowline" and "Where do you feel?"

"Snowline"

This poem compiles translations of François Villon's famous line: "Mais où sont les neiges d'antan?" (1461). Most are from complete translations of the untitled source poem, conventionally referred to as "Ballade des dames du temps jadis." See, for comparison, Caroline Bergvall's poem "VIA (48 Dante Variations)."

"Where do you feel?"

A poem of answers to the question "Where in your body do you feel grief, anxiety, and/or depression?" collected from social media, print, and personal sources. Deepest thanks to everyone who contributed. Several of the answers are my own.

THE POETS

BILLY-RAY BELCOURT is from the Driftpile Cree Nation. He is a Ph.D. student at the University of Alberta and a 2016 Rhodes Scholar who holds a M.St. in Women's Studies from the University of Oxford. In 2016, he was named one of six Indigenous writers to watch by CBC Books, and was the winner of the 2016 P. K. Page Founders' Award for Poetry. His work has been published in *Assaracus: A Journal of Gay Poetry, Decolonization, Red Rising Magazine, mâmawi-âcimowak, SAD Mag, Yellow Medicine Review, The Malahat Review, PRISM International*, and *The Next Quarterly*.

TONGO EISEN-MARTIN's previous book, the critically acclaimed *someone's dead already* (2015), was nominated for a California Book Award, and his poetry has been featured in *Harper's Magazine*. He is also a movement worker and educator who has taught in detention centres from New York's Rikers Island to California county jails. He has been a faculty member at the Institute for Research in African-American Studies at Columbia University, and his curriculum on the extrajudicial killing of Black people — "We Charge Genocide Again!" — has been used as an educational and organizing tool throughout America. He lives in San Francisco, California.

Author of more than a dozen books of poetry and two of literary criticism, SUSAN HOWE's recent collection of poems *That This* won the Bollingen Prize in 2011. Howe held the Samuel P. Capen Chair in Poetry and the Humanities at the State University of New York at Buffalo until her retirement in 2007. The recipient of a Guggenheim Fellowship, she was elected to the American Academy of Arts and Sciences in 1999 and served as a Chancellor to the Academy of American Poets from 2000 to 2006. In 2009 she was awarded a Fellowship to the American Academy at Berlin. Recently, she was an Artist-in-Residence at the Isabella Stewart Gardner Museum in Boston. Howe has also released three CDs in collaboration with the musician/composer David Grubbs, *Thiefth*, *Souls of the Labadie Tract*, and *Frolic Architecture*. In 2013 her word collages were exhibited at the Yale Union in Portland, Oregon, and in the Whitney Biennial Spring, 2014. Most recently, a limited press edition of *Tom Tit Tot* (word collages that amount to a series poem), with artwork by R. H. Quaytman, was published by MoMA in New York, and *Spontaneous Particulars: The Telepathy of Archives* by Christine Burgin and New Directions.

AISHA SASHA JOHN is a poet, dancer and choreographer. Her solo performance *The Aisha of Oz* premiered at the Whitney Museum in New York in 2017. Another iteration of the show will take place at the MAI in Montreal in 2018. Her previous poetry collection, *Thou* (2014), was a finalist for both the Trillium Book Award for Poetry and the ReLit Poetry Award. In addition to her solo work, she has choreographed, performed, and curated as a member of the performance collective WIVES. John's video work and text art have been exhibited in galleries and public installations. Born in Montreal, John has an M.F.A. in Creative Writing from the University of Guelph, and a B.A. in African Studies and Semiotics from the University of Toronto.

LAYLI LONG SOLDIER earned a B.F.A. from the Institute of American Indian Arts and an M.F.A. with honours from Bard College. She is the author of the chapbook *Chromosomory* (2010) and the full-length collection *Whereas* (2017), which was a finalist for the National Book Award. She has been a contributing editor to *Drunken Boat* and is poetry editor at Kore Press; in 2012, her participatory installation, *Whereas We Respond*, was featured on the Pine Ridge Reservation. In 2015, Long Soldier was awarded a National Artist Fellowship from the Native Arts and Cultures Foundation and a Lannan Literary Fellowship for Poetry. A citizen of the Oglala Lakota Nation, Long Soldier lives in Tsaile, Arizona, in the Navajo Nation, with her husband and daughter. She is an adjunct faculty member at Diné College.

The interdisciplinary practice of DONATO MANCINI focuses mainly on poetry, bookworks, text-based visual art, and cultural criticism. His books and chapbooks include *Snowline* (2015), *Loitersack* (2014), *Buffet World* (2011), *Fact 'N' Value* (2011), *Hell Passport no.22* (2008), *Æthel* (2007), *58 Free Coffees* (2006), and *Ligatures* (2005). *Ligatures* and *Æthel* were each nominated for the ReLit Poetry Award, and *Ligatures* received honourable mention in the Alcuin Society book design awards. Mancini's published critical writing includes work on the archive, time, and memory in *Anamnesia: Unforgetting* (2011), and a discourse analysis of poetry reviews in *You Must Work Harder to Write Poetry of Excellence* (2012). He holds a Ph.D. in English from the University of British Columbia.

NATALIE SHAPERO is the Professor of the Practice of Poetry at Tufts University and an editor at large of the *Kenyon Review*. Her first poetry collection, *No Object*, was published by Saturnalia Books in 2013. Shapero's writing has appeared in publications such as *The Nation*, *The New Republic*, *The New Yorker*, *Poetry*, and *The Progressive*. She holds degrees in creative writing and in law and has worked as a litigation fellow with Americans United for Separation of Church and State. Her awards include a National Endowment for the Arts Fellowship, a Ruth Lilly Fellowship, a *Kenyon Review* Fellowship, and a Great Lakes Colleges Association New Writers Award.

THE JUDGES

SARAH HOWE is a British poet, academic, and editor. Her first book, *Loop of Jade* (2015), won the T. S. Eliot Prize and the *Sunday Times* Young Writer of the Year Award. Born in Hong Kong to an English father and Chinese mother, she moved to England as a child. Her pamphlet *A Certain Chinese Encyclopedia* (2009) won an Eric Gregory Award from the Society of Authors. Howe is the founding editor of *Prac Crit*, an online journal of poetry and criticism. She held fellowships at the University of Cambridge, Harvard University's Radcliffe Institute, and University College London before recently taking up a lectureship in poetry at King's College London.

BEN LERNER is the author of three books of poetry (*The Lichtenberg Figures, Angle of Yaw,* and *Mean Free Path*), two novels (*Leaving the Atocha Station* and *10:04*), and a work of criticism (*The Hatred of Poetry*). He has received fellowships from the Fulbright, Guggenheim, and MacArthur Foundations, among many other honours.

IAN WILLIAMS is the author of *Personals*, shortlisted for the Griffin Poetry Prize and the Robert Kroetsch Poetry Book Award; *Not Anyone's Anything*, winner of the Danuta Gleed Literary Award for the best first collection of short fiction in Canada; and *You Know Who You Are*, a finalist for the ReLit Prize for poetry. His first novel, *Reproduction*, is forthcoming. He was named as one of ten Canadian writers to watch by the CBC. Williams completed his Ph.D. in English at the University of Toronto and teaches poetry in the Creative Writing Program at the University of British Columbia. He was the 2014-15 Canadian Writer-in-Residence for the University of Calgary's Distinguished Writers Program.

ACKNOWLEDGEMENTS

The publisher thanks the following for their kind permission to reprint the work contained in this volume:

"Faceless," "I have to talk to myself differently now," "Heaven Is All Goodbyes," and "Three buildings make a tide" from *Heaven Is All Goodbyes* by Tongo Eisen-Martin are reprinted by permission of City Lights.

"Epistolary Correspondences." and selections from "Titian Air Vent," "Tom Tit Tot," "Periscope," and "Debths" from *Debths* by Susan Howe are reprinted by permission of New Directions.

"My Hand and Cold," "Hard Child," "You Look Like I Feel," "Old Ad," "Teacup This," "Passing and Violence," and "Ten What" from *Hard Child* by Natalie Shapero are reprinted by permission of Copper Canyon Press.

"38" and selections from "Ȟe Sápa," "Vaporative," and "Whereas Statements" from *Whereas* by Layli Long Soldier are reprinted by permission of Graywolf Press.

"Gay Incantations," "The Rez Sisters II," "We Were Never Meant to Break Like This," "Grief After Grief After Grief After Grief (and endnotes), and selections from "The Oxford Journal"

THE GRIFFIN POETRY PRIZE
ANTHOLOGY 2018

The best books of poetry published in English internationally and in Canada are honoured each year with the $65,000 Griffin Poetry Prize, one of the world's most prestigious and richest international literary awards. Since 2001 this annual prize has acted as a tremendous spur to interest in and recognition of poetry, focusing worldwide attention on the formidable talent of poets writing in English and works in translation. And each year the editor of *The Griffin Poetry Prize Anthology* gathers the work of the extraordinary poets shortlisted for the awards, and introduces us to some of the finest poems in their collections.

This year, editor and prize juror Ian Williams's selections from the international shortlist include poems from Tongo Eisen-Martin's *Heaven Is All Goodbyes* (City Lights), Susan Howe's *Debths* (New Directions), Layli Long Soldier's *Whereas*, and Natalie Shapero's *Hard Child*. The selections from the Canadian shortlist include Billy-Ray Belcourt's *This Wound is a World*, Aisha Sasha John's *I have to live.*, and Donato Mancini's *Same Diff*.

In choosing the 2018 shortlist, prize jurors Sarah Howe, Ben Lerner, and Ian Williams each read 542 books of poetry, from 33 countries, including 17 translations. The jurors also wrote the citations that introduce the seven poets' nominated works.